I0427532

RISING

FROM THE

ASHES

RISING
FROM THE
ASHES

A COMPLETE GUIDE TO RECOVERING FROM
BUSINESS FAILURE AND GETTING BACK ON THE
ROAD TO SUCCESS

MOHAMED MAWJI

Other Books by Mohamed Mawji
The New Business Blueprint: A Step-by-Step Guide for Startup Success (2023)
Beyond Solutions: Mastering Outcomes for Sales Supremacy (2023)

© 2024 by Mohamed Mawji and EvolveBiz Inc. All rights reserved.

This book, **"Rising from the Ashes"** including all its contents and associated materials, is protected by copyright. No part of this publication may be reproduced, distributed, or transmitted in any form or by any means, including photocopying, recording, or other electronic or mechanical methods, without the prior written permission of the publisher, EvolveBiz, except in the case of brief quotations embodied in critical reviews and certain other noncommercial uses permitted by copyright law.

For permissions requests or inquiries, please contact: EvolveBiz Inc.- 2005 Tree Fork Lane. Unit 125, Longwood, Florida, 32750

Unauthorized use or reproduction of any part of this work is illegal and may be subject to civil and criminal penalties. The publisher and author assume no responsibility for errors, omissions, or damages caused by the use of the information contained in this book.

EvolveBiz Inc. and Mohamed Mawji are registered trademarks of their respective owners.

CONTENTS

This book **"Rising from the Ashes"** by Mohamed Mawji is an extensive and detailed exploration of various aspects crucial for business resilience and success. Here's a brief overview:

1. **Introduction:** The book begins with a powerful introduction to Mohamed Mawji, highlighting his journey and expertise in navigating the complex world of business, emphasizing the importance of learning from failures.

2. **Comprehensive Coverage:** The chapters cover a wide range of topics crucial for business resilience, such as financial management, team dynamics, customer service, data protection, and more. Each chapter delves into specific challenges businesses face and offers practical strategies for overcoming these hurdles.

3. **Real-world Insights and Quotes:** The book incorporates insightful quotes from notable figures and real-world examples, enriching the content with practical wisdom and relatable scenarios.

4. **Focus on Resilience Through Adversity:** A recurring theme is the emphasis on resilience, especially through economic downturns, operational inefficiencies, regulatory compliance issues, and the need for strategic pivoting in business.

5. **Holistic Approach to Business Management:** The guide takes a holistic approach, addressing not only financial and operational aspects but also delving into psychological factors, the impact of technology, and the importance of internal culture and team dynamics.

6. **Target Audience:** While the content is highly relevant to entrepreneurs and small to medium-sized enterprises (SMEs), its comprehensive nature makes it a valuable resource for any business professional seeking to understand and navigate the complexities of modern business landscapes.

7. **In-depth Analysis:** Each section provides in-depth analysis and actionable strategies, such as how to manage cash flow, navigate technological challenges, and maintain customer relationships during tough times.

8. **Practical Solutions and Tools:** The book doesn't just identify problems; it offers a range of solutions, tools, and strategies, empowering businesses to implement practical steps toward resilience and growth.

This guide is an excellent resource for business owners and entrepreneurs, offering insightful and practical advice for navigating the many challenges of running a business. The depth and breadth of the topics covered make it a comprehensive manual for business resilience.

WHO AM I TO AUTHOR THIS BOOK?

In the dynamic landscape of entrepreneurship, where the cacophony of challenges often overshadows the whispers of success, Mohamed Mawji stands as a luminary of insight and expertise. His entrepreneurial odyssey commenced at the youthful age of nineteen, marking the beginning of a remarkable journey through a diverse array of business endeavors. This journey, a harmonious interplay of setbacks and victories, has endowed Mohamed with a profound understanding of how to transform challenges into catalysts for success.

At the precipice of business failure, entrepreneurs often find themselves in a solitary struggle, grappling with the daunting prospect of collapse. It is in these moments of isolation and uncertainty that "Rising from the Ashes" emerges as an indispensable companion. This book, borne of Mohamed's extensive experience, is a beacon of hope and guidance, illuminating the path back to success.

Mohamed's acumen encompasses the entire gamut of business dynamics – from the nascent stages of startups to the complexities of operational management, financial stewardship, and the nuanced strategies of growth and change management. His journey through various business cycles provides a panoramic view of business evolution, from the era of Digital Enterprise Minicomputers and CP/M-based desktop computers to the modern epoch of handheld devices like iPhones and iPads, and the transformative power of Artificial Intelligence in enhancing business efficiency and precision.

This book is more than a mere anthology of experiences; it is a heartfelt initiative by Mohamed to mentor and assist aspiring entrepreneurs. Through "Rising from the Ashes," he offers wisdom and practical strategies to help floundering businesses regain their footing and achieve success. He shares invaluable lessons from his encounters with both adversity and triumph, presenting them as a navigational compass for the exhilarating journey of entrepreneurship.

The dedication of this book to Mohamed's spouse is a poignant acknowledgment of the critical role played by unwavering support in an entrepreneur's journey. It highlights the importance of resilience and understanding, not only in professional endeavors but also in the sanctuaries of personal life. With an open heart and a generous spirit, Mohamed extends his guidance through this book, empowering emerging entrepreneurs to embrace their failures, learn from them, and emerge victorious in the ever-evolving world of business.

Mohamed Mawji

"Failure isn't fatal, but failure to change might be." —*John Wooden*

"Success consists of going from failure to failure without loss of enthusiasm." —*Winston Churchill*

"A person who doubts himself is like a man who would enlist in the ranks of his enemies and bear arms against himself. He makes his failure certain by himself being the first person to be convinced of it." —*Alexandre Dumas*

"Only those who dare to fail greatly can ever achieve greatly." —*Robert F. Kennedy*

"A man may fall many times, but he won't be a failure until he says that someone pushed him." —*Elmer G. Letterman*

"There are no failures–just experiences and your reactions to them." —*Tom Krause*

"Failure and Inventions are Inseparable Twins" – Jeff Bezos

"Fear is linked to Failure" – Imam Ali (AS)

"It is impossible to live without failing at something unless you live so cautiously that you might as well not have lived at all. In which case, you fail by default" – J.K. Rowling

FORWARD

Embracing Resilience in the Face of Challenges

In the ever-changing landscape of entrepreneurship, failure is a word often whispered in hushed tones. It's the shadow that looms over our aspirations, the specter we strive to avoid at all costs. But what if I told you that within failure lies an untapped wellspring of growth, innovation, and resilience? This is precisely the transformative journey that "Rising from the Ashes" embarks upon.

In these pages, you will find a refreshing perspective—one that doesn't shy away from challenges but invites you to embrace them. Authored by the insightful Mohamed Mawji, this book is not just a guide; it's a testament to the power of entrepreneurial spirit, the tenacity to learn from setbacks, and the ability to evolve through adversity.

As someone who has witnessed the entrepreneurial journey's ebbs and flows, I can attest that the wisdom contained within these chapters is not just theoretical; its battle tested. Mohamed Mawji, a luminary in the business realm, brings a wealth of experience and a keen understanding of the dynamics that define resilience. He doesn't just talk about resilience; he embodies it.

"Rising from the Ashes" is a roadmap, a companion for those who dare to dream, who venture into the world of business with the knowledge that challenges are not obstacles but steppingstones. It's a guide for entrepreneurs, leaders, and visionaries who understand that failure is not a verdict but a catalyst for growth.

This book doesn't just explore the intricacies of business failure; it equips you with the tools to navigate them. From financial insights to operational excellence, from leadership acumen to strategic adaptability, each chapter offers a beacon of light in the darkest of entrepreneurial storms.

As you embark on this transformative journey, remember that resilience is not the absence of challenges but the ability to evolve through them. It's the spirit that turns setbacks into setups for success. "Rising from the Ashes" is not just a book; it's your compass on this voyage—a compass that points not only to triumph but to lasting resilience.

May your journey through these pages inspire you, challenge you, and ultimately, empower you to evolve through failure. For within the crucible of adversity lies the alchemy of resilience, and it's a journey well worth taking.

INTRODUCTION

Navigating the Complex Tapestry of Business Failure

In the quiet corridors of entrepreneurship, where the echoes of success are drowned by the ominous whispers of failure, there exists a moment more harrowing than any other—a moment when the realization crystallizes that the business, the vessel you've captained with passion and sweat, may be on the precipice of collapse. It is a plunge into the abyss, a descent into the worst chapter of an entrepreneur's career.

Yet, as we stand on the brink of this abyss, it is not the specter of failure that shadows our every move. No, it is the nuanced dance with change, a subtle choreography of evolution, which eludes many. The unyielding principles of business, stoic in their constancy, endure regardless of the industry embarked upon.

Consider the first sentinel, Money—the lifeblood coursing through the veins of commerce. In 1960, the pulse was no different than today. Funding, financial vigilance, and accounting precision remain the sine qua non of a thriving enterprise. But why, then, do stalwart businesses falter? The culprit often lurks in an inability to grasp the shifting sands of commerce, a failure to evolve. Business, like a chameleon, must

1

change its hues with the times—swiftly, seamlessly, almost automated.

Then, there is Team—the symphony of skill, the architects of success. Your business, they say, is only as robust as the team propelling it forward. Like threading delicate cotton through a sewing needle by hand, the task of aligning skill sets and personal strengths with organizational needs demands finesse. Retention, the linchpin, hinges on a philosophy woven with threads of ongoing training, welfare, job security, and the unshakeable confidence in a leader and the company's continuity.

Failure, the ominous specter, is not the unequivocal end. It is, instead, a crossroads where the decision to abandon the quest for success is made—a choice forged either in the crucible of early adversity or after exhaustive battles against the headwinds of recovery.

In the ensuing chapters, we dissect the vulnerable sinews of failure, exploring the intricacies of collapse, recovery, and the delicate dance with time. For, in those moments of despair, what emerges as paramount is the relentless pursuit of recovery—the resilience to mend what is broken and reclaim the trajectory toward success.

As we navigate the tumultuous waters of entrepreneurship, let us reflect upon the wisdom of those who have faced the abyss and emerged stronger. In the words of John Wooden, "Failure isn't fatal, but failure to change might be." It is a clarion call to evolve or face obsolescence—a sentiment echoed by the resounding words of Jeff Bezos, "Failure and inventions are inseparable twins."

And so, as we embark on this journey of introspection, let us draw inspiration from the luminaries who have treaded this path before us. In the words of J.K. Rowling, "It is impossible to live without failing at something unless you live so cautiously that you might as well not have lived at all. In which case, you fail by default." Embrace the challenge, for in the crucible of failure lies the forge of true success.

THE PRACTICAL REALITIES OF SMALL ENTERPRISES

To begin, let's address the challenging aspects often faced by small businesses, acknowledging the obstacles that can impede the entrepreneurial spirit behind establishing new ventures worldwide. The path to success can be perilous, with high stakes for those embarking on the journey of starting and sustaining a small business.

The foremost reason behind many business struggles is inadequate cash flow. However, this is not the only culprit; other prominent factors contributing to small business failures include:

- 79% fail due to initial undercapitalization.
- 78% falter without a comprehensive business plan, lacking in-depth research.
- 77% stumbled due to improper pricing strategies, overlooking essential factors.
- 73% are tripped up by overoptimistic projections for sales, finances, and success prerequisites.
- 70% falter due to an inability to recognize and address weaknesses, hesitating to seek external assistance. (Source: Investopedia)

Exploring these common pitfalls further will be the focus of the next chapter. The daunting statistics often lead small business owners to lose confidence, prompting premature surrender rather than persevering through adversity. However, resilience in the face of such challenges is often the key to eventual success.

WHY RECOGNIZING EARLY INDICATORS MATTERS: NAVIGATING THE PATH TO BUSINESS SURVIVAL

In the intricate dance of business, recognizing the early indicators of failure is akin to reading the signs of an impending storm at sea. It is not merely a matter of vigilance; it's a critical skill that can determine the survival or demise of a business. This chapter explores the profound importance of early detection, emphasizing why business owners and leaders must be attuned to these warning signals.

1. **The Significance of Early Detection: A Business Compass**
   Navigating Uncharted Waters: Business landscapes are dynamic, with ever-changing currents influenced by market trends, customer behaviors, and external forces. Early indicators function as a compass, providing a sense of direction amid uncertainty. Recognizing warning signs enables businesses to plot a course, avoiding potential pitfalls and charting a path towards sustainable success.

   Proactive Problem Solving: Early detection is not merely about identifying problems; it's about proactively solving them. It grants business leaders the foresight to address underlying issues before they escalate. This proactive stance is akin to preemptive navigation, steering the business away from storms before they unleash their full force.

2. The Gradual Decline Trap: A Warning to Heed

Silent Erosion of Viability: Ignoring early indicators can lead to a gradual decline, akin to the erosion of a coastline. What might start as a small crack in the business foundation can, over time, widen into a chasm that becomes insurmountable. Recognizing the subtle signs prevents the silent erosion of a business's viability.

The Irreversibility Quandary: A gradual decline, when left unchecked, can reach a point of irreversibility. It transforms what could have been manageable challenges into insurmountable obstacles. Early recognition is the key to breaking free from this quandary, offering the opportunity to implement corrective measures while there's still room for maneuvering.

3. The Future Viability of the Business: A Stakes Game

Strategic Decision-Making: Early detection equips business owners with the insights needed for strategic decision-making. It transforms uncertainty into a calculated game where each move is informed by an understanding of the playing field. The future viability of the business becomes a stakes game, and recognizing early indicators is the currency for making informed bets.

Paving the Path to Recovery: Beyond survival, early recognition lays the foundation for recovery. It transforms a crisis into an opportunity for renewal and growth. Armed with knowledge, leaders can pivot towards a path of recovery, steering the business away from the brink and towards a brighter future.

4. **A Preview of Chapters to Come: Strategies and Tools**

Assessing Different Facets: The subsequent chapters promise a deep dive into specific strategies and tools for assessing various facets of a business. From financial health to operational efficiency, market analysis to leadership evaluation, each chapter will unravel a layer of the business landscape, empowering leaders to make informed decisions.

Empowering Business Leaders: These chapters are more than just a toolkit; they serve as a guide for business leaders to navigate the complexities of their enterprises. By understanding and applying the strategies presented, leaders can uncover the hidden intricacies of their businesses, making the invisible visible and transforming challenges into opportunities.

CONCLUSION: EARLY RECOGNITION AS A BEACON OF HOPE

In the vast ocean of business, early recognition serves as a beacon of hope, illuminating the way forward for business owners and leaders. This chapter underscores the profound importance of recognizing early indicators, likening it to navigating uncharted waters. As we embark on a journey through the subsequent chapters, we invite business leaders to hone their skills in deciphering the signs that shape the destiny of their enterprises. The ability to read the currents of change and foresee challenges is not just a skill; it is a survival instinct.

Through the chapters that follow, we aim to equip business leaders with the knowledge and tools to not only recognize early indicators, but to steer their companies away from failure and toward a path of recovery and enduring success.

THE EVOLVEBIZ RESILIENCE TOOLKIT

Preventative Measures
- Regularly analyze and update business strategies.
- Maintain a healthy cash reserve.
- Invest in employee training and development.
- Conduct frequent market research to stay ahead of trends.

During a Crisis
- Rapidly assess the situation and its impact on the business.
- Communicate transparently with stakeholders.
- Pivot business strategies if necessary.
- Seek advice from mentors, experts, or consultants.

Post-Failure Recovery
- Conduct a thorough analysis of what led to the failure.
- Re-evaluate and adjust business plans and strategies.
- Rebuild a strong, committed team.
- Focus on building a resilient organizational culture.

Sustaining Growth
- Continuously monitor and adapt to market changes.
- Foster innovation and encourage new ideas.

- Regularly review financial health and business metrics.
- Engage in community and network building for broader perspectives.

Long-term Resilience
- Develop a long-term vision that accommodates change.
- Build strong relationships with customers and suppliers.
- Staying informed about technological advancements and integrating them was beneficial.
- Regularly revisit and update the business continuity plan.

This comprehensive analysis and checklist provide a structured approach to understanding and implementing the principles of business resilience. It serves as a practical guide for entrepreneurs and business leaders to navigate through challenges and position their businesses for long-term success.

SELF-ASSESSMENT TOOL FRAMEWORK

PART 1: BUSINESS RESILIENCE EVALUATION

1. Adaptability Assessment:

- Rate your business's ability to adapt to changes in the market (1-5).
- Reflect on recent instances where your business had to pivot or adjust strategies.
- Identify areas where adaptability can be improved.

2. Financial Health Check:

- Assess your current financial stability (1-5).
- Review cash flow, profit margins, and debt levels.
- Pinpoint financial management areas needing attention.

3. Team Strength and Culture Analysis:

- Evaluate the strength of your team and company culture (1-5).
- Consider aspects like team collaboration, morale, and skills alignment with company goals.
- Identify opportunities for team development and culture enhancement.

PART 2: RECOVERY AND GROWTH STRATEGIES

4. Crisis Management Proficiency:

- How effectively can your business respond to unexpected crises? (1-5)
- Review past responses to crises for insights.
- Develop a plan to improve crisis response.

5. Innovation and Improvement Gauge:

- Rate your business's innovation efforts (1-5).
- Examine recent innovations or improvements made in your business.
- Plan actions to foster a more innovative environment.

6. Customer Engagement and Feedback:

- Assess how well your business engages with and listens to customers (1-5).
- Consider customer feedback mechanisms and engagement strategies.
- Develop a plan to enhance customer relationships.

PART 3: LONG-TERM SUCCESS AND SUSTAINABILITY

7. Market Trends and Future Preparedness:

- How well is your business prepared for future market trends? (1-5)
- Analyze how current trends might impact your business.
- Plan how to align your business with future trends.

8. Sustainability and Growth Plans:

- Rate your business's sustainability and long-term growth plans (1-5).
- Review your business plan for long-term viability.
- Identify areas where the business can be more sustainable.

9. Continuous Learning and Development:

- Evaluate the emphasis on learning and development in your business (1-5).
- Consider how learning and development are encouraged.
- Plan to integrate continuous learning into your business strategy.

SCORING AND INTERPRETATION

- **35-45**: High Resilience - Your business demonstrates strong resilience and adaptability.
- **25-34**: Moderate Resilience - Some areas are well-managed, but there's room for improvement.
- **15-24**: Low Resilience - Critical need to develop resilience strategies.
- **Below 15**: Urgent Action Needed - Immediate focus required on resilience and adaptability.

15-24: LOW RESILIENCE

Critical need to develop resilience strategies.

For businesses that have identified themselves as having **low resilience,** based on the self-assessment tool in "Evolving Through Failure," it's crucial to develop and implement resilience strategies urgently. Here's a comprehensive analysis and action plan tailored for such businesses:

Comprehensive Analysis for Low Resilience Businesses

1. Key Vulnerabilities Identified:
- Difficulty in adapting to market changes.
- Weak financial health and management.
- Team dynamics and culture are not conducive to resilience.
- Inadequate crisis management strategies.
- Low innovation and poor customer engagement.
- Lack of preparedness for future market trends.
- Insufficient focus on sustainability and long-term growth.

2. Underlying Causes:
- Ineffective leadership and management practices.
- Lack of a clear, adaptable business strategy.
- Inadequate resource allocation to critical areas.
- Poor communication within the organization.
- Limited understanding of market dynamics and customer needs.

Action Plan for Building Resilience

Step 1: Strengthen Leadership and Management
- **Objective**: Enhance leadership skills and develop effective management practices.
- **Actions**:
- Engage in leadership training programs.
- Foster a culture of open communication and feedback.
- Implement regular team meetings and strategy sessions.

Step 2: Develop a Flexible Business Strategy
- **Objective**: Create an adaptable business plan that can withstand market fluctuations.

- **Actions**:
- Conduct a thorough market analysis.
- Involve team members in strategy development for diverse perspectives.
- Regularly review and adjust the business plan as needed.

Step 3: Improve Financial Management

- **Objective**: Establish robust financial practices for better stability.
- **Actions**:
- Consult with a financial advisor or accountant.
- Implement budgeting and cash flow management tools.
- Diversify revenue streams and explore new funding options.

Step 4: Enhance Team Dynamics and Culture

- **Objective**: Build a strong, collaborative, and resilient team.
- **Actions**:
- Conduct team-building activities and workshops.
- Promote a culture of continuous learning and development.
- Encourage innovation and creativity within the team.

Step 5: Implement Effective Crisis Management

- **Objective**: Prepare the business to manage crises efficiently.
- **Actions**:
- Develop a comprehensive crisis management plan.
- Conduct regular crisis simulation exercises.
- Set up a crisis response team.

Step 6: Boost Innovation and Customer Engagement

- **Objective**: Foster innovation and strengthen customer relationships.

- **Actions**:
- Invest in research and development.
- Enhance customer feedback mechanisms.
- Implement customer-centric strategies.

Step 7: Plan for Future Trends and Sustainability

- **Objective**: Align the business with future market trends and sustainability.
- **Actions**:
- Stay updated with industry trends and forecasts.
- Incorporate sustainable practices into business operations.
- Plan for long-term growth and scalability.

Monitoring and Evaluation

- **Regular Check-Ins**: Schedule monthly reviews to assess progress.
- **KPI Tracking**: Use Key Performance Indicators (KPIs) to measure improvements in each area.
- **Adaptation**: Be prepared to adjust the plan based on feedback and results.

BELOW 15: URGENT ACTION NEEDED

Immediate focus required on resilience and adaptability.

For businesses scoring below 15 in the self-assessment, indicating an urgent need for action in resilience and adaptability, a comprehensive and immediate action plan is essential. Here's a detailed analysis and action plan tailored for such situations:

Comprehensive Analysis for Businesses with Urgent Action Needed

1. Critical Weaknesses Identified:

- Severe difficulty in adapting to market changes and challenges.
- Significantly poor financial health and management practices.
- Lack of effective leadership and cohesive team culture.
- Inadequate crisis management and innovation strategies.
- Neglect in understanding and engaging with customer needs.
- Lack of preparedness for future market trends and sustainability.

2. Root Causes:

- Absence of a clear, strategic direction and business planning.
- Ineffective or absent financial planning and risk management.
- Poor organizational structure and internal communication.
- Resistance to change and innovation within the organization.
- Limited engagement with market realities and customer feedback.

ACTION PLAN FOR URGENT IMPROVEMENT

Immediate Steps (0-3 Months)

- **Conduct an Emergency Business Review**:
- Bring together key stakeholders for an in-depth analysis of the business's current state.
- Identify immediate threats and viable opportunities for quick wins.

- **Establish Crisis Management Protocols**:
- Create a crisis response team and develop basic crisis management plans.
- Conduct immediate risk assessment to prioritize areas of concern.
- **Implement Basic Financial Controls**:
- Introduce fundamental financial tracking and management tools.
- Focus on critical financial issues like cash flow management and cost reduction.

Short-term Goals (3-6 Months)

- **Develop a Flexible Business Strategy**:
- Start building a more adaptable business plan, considering market research and trends.
- Set short-term goals that are achievable and measurable.
- **Strengthen Leadership and Team Dynamics**:
- Begin leadership development programs.
- Initiate regular team meetings and communication channels.
- **Enhance Customer Engagement**:
- Implement basic customer feedback mechanisms.
- Start incorporating customer insights into business decisions.

Medium-term Objectives (6-12 Months)

- **Build Comprehensive Resilience Plans**:
- Develop detailed plans for business resilience and adaptability.
- Regularly review and update these plans based on market changes.
- **Foster a Culture of Innovation**:

- Encourage innovation through workshops, brainstorming sessions, and incentives.
- Implement processes to continuously improve products/services based on feedback.
- **Plan for Sustainability and Long-term Growth**:
- Lay the groundwork for sustainable business practices.
- Begin planning for long-term growth, scalability, and market expansion.

Long-term Strategies (1 Year and Beyond)

- **Implement Robust Financial Management Systems**:
- Establish advanced financial planning, budgeting, and forecasting systems.
- Regularly review financial performance against industry benchmarks.
- **Develop Advanced Crisis Management and Innovation Systems**:
- Create detailed crisis management frameworks.
- Invest in research and development for sustained innovation.
- **Engage in Continuous Market Analysis and Adaptation**:
- Maintain ongoing market analysis to stay ahead of trends.
- Continuously adapt business strategies to align with market needs.

Monitoring, Evaluation, and Adjustment

- **Regular Performance Reviews**:
- Conduct frequent reviews to monitor progress and identify areas needing attention.
- Use KPIs and feedback to measure the effectiveness of implemented strategies.
- **Adaptive Planning**:

- Be prepared to adjust plans based on performance reviews and external changes.
- Foster a mindset of continuous learning and adaptation within the organization.

This action plan is designed to systematically address the areas of weakness identified in the self-assessment, leading to the development of a more resilient business structure. It's important for businesses with low resilience to act decisively and commit to ongoing improvements to build a solid foundation for future success.

DEFINING BUSINESS FAILURE:

Business failure can be broadly defined as the inability of a company to meet its financial obligations and sustain profitable operations. It goes beyond mere financial losses; it encompasses a breakdown in various aspects of a business, leading to an inability to thrive or survive in the market. This breakdown can manifest in several ways, such as declining revenues, eroding market share, operational inefficiencies, and a compromised ability to adapt to changing business landscapes.

Cash Flow Issues: The Silent Killer - Unraveling the Tangled Web
Cash flow issues represent a pervasive challenge for small businesses, often manifesting as a silent killer that gradually erodes financial stability. A deeper dive into this predicament reveals that cash flow troubles extend beyond a mere lack of liquidity; they intricately weave through multiple facets of business operations, creating bottlenecks at both ends of the sales and purchasing spectrum.

1. Vendor Relations: A Delicate Balancing Act
The Challenge: Small businesses heavily reliant on suppliers face a precarious balancing act. The need to secure raw

materials, goods, or services from vendors is constant, but when cash flow is constrained, timely payments to suppliers become challenging.

Impact:
- **Strained Relationships:** Delays in payments strain relationships with suppliers, potentially jeopardizing the reliability of the supply chain.
- **Reduced Negotiation Power:** The ability to negotiate favorable terms with suppliers diminishes, as cash-strapped businesses are often compelled to accept less favorable payment terms.

Strategies for Mitigation:
- **Transparent Communication:** Open and transparent communication about financial constraints can foster understanding with vendors.
- **Negotiation Skills:** Sharpening negotiation skills can help in securing extended payment terms or discounts during challenging periods.
- **Strategic Inventory Management:** Efficient inventory management reduces the need for large upfront payments and helps in maintaining good relations with suppliers.

2. Inventory Management: The Symbiotic Connection

The Challenge: Inventory is a double-edged sword. On one hand, it ties up cash, and on the other, inadequate stock levels can lead to missed sales opportunities. For small businesses, striking the right balance is crucial, but cash flow limitations can disrupt this equilibrium.

Impact:

- **Overstocking and Cash Drain:** Insufficient cash may force businesses to maintain lean inventories, risking stockouts and lost sales.
- **Missed Sales Opportunities:** On the flip side, inadequate inventory levels due to cash constraints can result in missed sales opportunities.

Strategies for Mitigation:

- **Just-in-Time Inventory:** Adopting a just-in-time inventory management approach minimizes excess stock, reducing the strain on cash reserves.
- **Forecasting Accuracy:** Improve demand forecasting accuracy to align inventory levels with anticipated sales, preventing overstocking or stockouts.
- **Negotiate Favorable Terms with Suppliers:** Negotiate flexible payment terms with suppliers to align with sales cycles and reduce the impact on cash flow.

3. Sales and Purchasing Bottlenecks: The Vicious Cycle

The Challenge: Cash flow issues create a vicious cycle, forming bottlenecks in both sales and purchasing processes. As businesses struggle to meet financial obligations, the entire operational cycle, from procuring goods to making sales, experiences disruptions.

Impact:

- **Delayed Purchases:** Inability to pay suppliers on time leads to delayed purchases, affecting the availability of goods for sale.
- **Restricted Sales:** Limited inventory due to cash constraints restricts sales, exacerbating cash flow challenges.

Strategies for Mitigation:

- **Integrated Systems:** Implement integrated systems that streamline sales and purchasing processes, providing real-time visibility into cash flow.
- **Flexible Payment Terms:** Work with suppliers and customers to establish flexible payment terms that align with the business's cash flow dynamics.
- **Short-Term Financing Options:** Explore short-term financing options, such as lines of credit, to bridge temporary gaps in cash flow and keep the operational cycle running smoothly.

4. **Cash Flow Forecasting: Navigating the Financial Landscape**
   The Challenge: Many small businesses lack comprehensive cash flow forecasting mechanisms. Without a clear understanding of future cash inflows and outflows, businesses are ill-equipped to proactively address potential challenges.

Impact:

- **Reactive Decision-Making:** Without accurate cash flow forecasts, businesses are forced into a reactive stance, addressing issues only when they become critical.
- **Missed Growth Opportunities:** Inability to anticipate cash flow gaps may result in missed opportunities for business expansion or strategic investments.

Strategies for Mitigation:

- **Regular Forecasting:** Implement regular cash flow forecasting to anticipate and plan for future financial needs.

- **Scenario Analysis:** Conduct scenario analyses to assess the impact of various factors on cash flow and develop contingency plans.
- **Use of Technology:** Leverage financial management software and tools that provide real-time insights into cash flow dynamics.

CONCLUSION: MASTERING THE CASH FLOW CHESSBOARD

Navigating cash flow challenges requires businesses to master the intricate chessboard of financial management. By addressing issues at the intersection of vendor relations, inventory management, and the operational cycle, businesses can break free from the silent killer's grip. Transparent communication, strategic negotiations, and leveraging technology are essential tools in this financial chess match, enabling small businesses to not only survive but thrive in the ever-evolving business landscape.

MARKET DEMAND AND COMPETITION

Sustaining Success Beyond Competitive Pricing

Navigating the competitive landscape successfully involves more than offering competitive prices. Even when customers are eager to buy, and your pricing aligns well with competitors, sustaining success requires a multifaceted strategy that goes beyond cost considerations. Here's a deeper dive into key aspects to consider:

1. Understanding Customer Needs: The Heart of Value Proposition

The Challenge: Even with competitive pricing, businesses must continuously understand and meet customer needs. A lack of alignment with customer expectations can erode brand loyalty, irrespective of pricing advantages.

Strategies:

- **Customer Surveys and Feedback:** Regularly solicit feedback from customers through surveys and reviews to understand their evolving needs.
- **Market Research:** Invest in ongoing market research to stay abreast of industry trends and changing consumer preferences.

- **Personalization:** Tailor products, services, and marketing approaches to cater to specific customer segments.

2. Brand Differentiation: Beyond Price Tags

The Challenge: In a crowded marketplace, standing out requires more than competitive prices. Building a strong brand identity that resonates with customers is crucial for long-term success.

Strategies:
- **Brand Storytelling:** Develop a compelling brand narrative that goes beyond products or services, connecting emotionally with customers.
- **Unique Value Proposition:** Clearly communicate what sets your brand apart, whether it's exceptional customer service, superior product quality, or a commitment to sustainability.
- **Consistent Branding:** Ensure consistency in branding across all touchpoints, fostering recognition and trust.

3. Customer Experience Excellence: Turning Buyers into Advocates

The Challenge: A positive customer experience is a powerful differentiator. Even with competitive prices, if the customer journey is lacking, businesses risk losing customers to competitors offering a superior experience.

Strategies:
- **Invest in Training:** Train and empower employees to deliver exceptional customer service.
- **Omni-Channel Presence:** Provide a seamless experience across online and offline channels.

- **Post-Purchase Engagement:** Foster ongoing relationships with customers through follow-ups, loyalty programs, and personalized communications.

4. Innovation and Adaptability: Staying Ahead of Trends

The Challenge: Competitive pricing alone won't secure long-term success. Businesses need to innovate and adapt to changing market dynamics, ensuring they stay relevant to customers.

Strategies:

- **R&D Investments:** Allocate resources to research and development to continually improve products or services.
- **Agile Business Practices:** Foster a culture of adaptability, enabling the business to pivot in response to emerging trends.
- **Technology Adoption:** Embrace new technologies that enhance products, services, or the overall customer experience.

5. Strategic Marketing: Beyond Price Promotion

The Challenge: Marketing is more than just promoting prices. Businesses need a holistic marketing strategy that encompasses brand-building, customer engagement, and targeted promotional efforts.

Strategies:

- **Content Marketing:** Create valuable and engaging content that establishes your brand as an authority in the industry.
- **Social Media Engagement:** Leverage social media platforms to connect with customers, share brand stories, and gather feedback.

- **Segmented Campaigns:** Tailor marketing campaigns to specific customer segments, addressing their unique needs and preferences.

6. Aggressive Competitor Analysis: Staying Informed
The Challenge: Even when your pricing is competitive, a lack of awareness about competitor strategies can pose risks. Businesses must actively monitor the competitive landscape.

Strategies:
- **Competitor Benchmarks:** Regularly benchmark your products, services, and pricing against key competitors.
- **SWOT Analysis:** Conduct regular SWOT analyses to identify strengths, weaknesses, opportunities, and threats in comparison to competitors.
- **Market Intelligence Tools:** Utilize market intelligence tools to stay updated on competitor activities, pricing changes, and market trends.

7. Building Partnerships: Expanding Reach
The Challenge: Collaborative partnerships can enhance a business's reach and offerings. A failure to explore partnership opportunities may limit growth potential.

Strategies:
- **Identify Complementary Businesses:** Seek partnerships with businesses that offer complementary products or services.
- **Joint Marketing Initiatives:** Collaborate on marketing campaigns or events to reach a broader audience.
- **Leverage Industry Networks:** Engage with industry networks and associations to explore partnership opportunities.

8. **Sustainability and Corporate Social Responsibility: Meeting Ethical Expectations**

The Challenge: Modern consumers increasingly value businesses that demonstrate a commitment to sustainability and corporate social responsibility (CSR). Ignoring these aspects may impact brand perception.

Strategies:

- **Environmental Initiatives:** Implement eco-friendly practices in operations and communicate these efforts to customers.
- **Community Engagement:** Participate in community-oriented initiatives that align with CSR goals.
- **Transparent Communication:** Clearly communicate the business's commitment to sustainability and ethical practices.

CONCLUSION: BEYOND PRICE WARS TO LASTING SUCCESS

While competitive pricing is a crucial aspect of market success, sustaining that success requires a holistic approach that encompasses customer understanding, brand differentiation, exceptional customer experiences, innovation, strategic marketing, competitor analysis, partnerships, and a commitment to ethical business practices. By navigating the competitive landscape with a comprehensive strategy, businesses can position themselves not just as cost-effective options but as enduring choices that cater to the diverse and evolving needs of their customers.

MANAGEMENT AND LEADERSHIP PROBLEMS

Navigating the Critical Path

Management and leadership play a pivotal role in shaping the destiny of a business. When challenges arise, it is imperative for owners, entrepreneurs, and executives to navigate the intricate landscape of leadership with a blend of realism, emotional intelligence, and a commitment to informed decision-making.

1. **Embracing Reality: A Leadership Imperative**
   The Challenge: In the face of adversity, leaders must confront reality head-on. This requires a candid assessment of the business's current state, acknowledging weaknesses, and recognizing areas that demand improvement.

Strategies:
- **Open Communication Channels:** Foster an organizational culture that encourages open communication and honest feedback.
- **Data-Driven Assessments:** Base evaluations on factual data rather than assumptions or wishful thinking.

- **Leadership Transparency:** Be transparent about challenges and avoid sugarcoating issues to maintain trust within the team.

2. Dismissing Emotional Biases: The Rational Leader

The Challenge: While it's natural for owners and executives to have emotional attachments to their businesses, effective leadership demands a degree of emotional detachment. Decisions made in the heat of emotions can be detrimental to the overall health of the business.

Strategies:

- **Self-Awareness:** Leaders must be self-aware, recognizing their emotional triggers and biases.
- **Objective Decision-Making:** Encourage a decision-making process based on objective analysis rather than emotional reactions.
- **Constructive Feedback:** Seek feedback from trusted advisors or colleagues who can provide impartial perspectives.

3. Investigating with Intelligence: Root Cause Analysis

The Challenge: Identifying the root causes of challenges requires a systematic and intelligent approach. Jumping to conclusions or placing blame without a thorough investigation can exacerbate problems.

Strategies:

- **Root Cause Analysis:** Conduct a comprehensive analysis to identify the underlying factors contributing to challenges.
- **Data-Backed Insights:** Rely on data and evidence to inform decisions rather than relying solely on anecdotes or assumptions.

- **Expert Consultation:** Engage with industry experts or consultants to gain insights beyond the internal perspective.

4. Taking Ownership: A Mark of Leadership Maturity

The Challenge: Effective leaders take ownership of both successes and failures. This accountability fosters a culture of responsibility within the organization.

Strategies:
- **Transparent Leadership:** Acknowledge mistakes openly and communicate the steps being taken to address them.
- **Leading by Example:** Demonstrate accountability in your own actions, setting a precedent for the rest of the team.
- **Ownership Mentality:** Instill a sense of ownership throughout the organization, encouraging employees to take responsibility for their roles.

5. Peaceful Resolution: Conflict Management Skills

The Challenge: Leadership challenges often come with interpersonal conflicts. Managing these conflicts peacefully is crucial for maintaining a healthy work environment.

Strategies:
- **Active Listening:** Develop active listening skills to understand the perspectives of all parties involved.
- **Mediation:** When conflicts arise, function as a mediator to facilitate constructive conversations and resolutions.
- **Conflict Resolution Training:** Provide training for leaders on conflict resolution techniques and strategies.

6. Cultivating Emotional Intelligence: The Heart of Leadership

The Challenge: Leaders with high emotional intelligence are better equipped to navigate challenges. Developing this skill set is essential for effective leadership.

Strategies:
- **Self-Reflection:** Regularly reflect on emotional responses and their impact on decision-making.
- **Empathy:** Cultivate empathy toward the experiences and perspectives of others.
- **Emotional Intelligence Training:** Provide training opportunities for leaders to enhance their emotional intelligence.

7. Strategic Planning for Recovery: The Roadmap Ahead

The Challenge: Leadership in times of crisis requires a strategic recovery plan. This plan should encompass short-term solutions and long-term strategies for sustainable success.

Strategies:
- **Scenario Planning:** Anticipate potential future scenarios and develop contingency plans.
- **Goal Alignment:** Align recovery strategies with the long-term goals of the business.
- **Adaptive Leadership:** Embrace adaptive leadership, adjusting strategies based on evolving circumstances.

CONCLUSION: GUIDING THE SHIP THROUGH STORMY SEAS

In the realm of management and leadership, the journey through challenges demands a captain who can navigate the ship with clarity, intelligence, and emotional resilience. By embracing reality, dismissing emotional biases, conducting intelligent investigations, taking ownership, managing conflicts peacefully, cultivating emotional intelligence, and strategically planning for recovery, leaders can guide their organizations through stormy seas, emerging stronger on the other side. Leadership is not just about steering the ship; it's about ensuring its seaworthiness and the well-being of its crew.

NAVIGATING THE MARKET

The Critical Role of Planning and Strategy in Business Success

L ack of planning and strategy is akin to setting sail without a map in uncharted waters. The absence of a well-defined roadmap leaves businesses vulnerable to the unpredictable currents of the market. Let's delve into the critical aspects of planning and strategy and explore how small businesses can navigate the path forward with purpose and resilience.

1. The Significance of Planning: A North Star for Business

The Challenge: In the absence of a clear plan, businesses operate in a state of uncertainty. The lack of direction hinders the ability to make informed decisions and compromises the overall vision for growth.

Strategies:
- **Comprehensive Business Plan:** Develop a comprehensive business plan outlining the mission, vision, goals, and strategies for achieving them.
- **SWOT Analysis:** Conduct a SWOT analysis (Strengths, Weaknesses, Opportunities, Threats) to identify internal and external factors affecting the business.

- **Long-Term Vision:** Define a long-term vision that provides a sense of purpose and direction for the entire organization.

2. Strategic Vision: Beyond Survival to Thriving

The Challenge: Survival mode is not a sustainable business strategy. Small businesses need a strategic vision that extends beyond immediate challenges and focuses on long-term sustainability.

Strategies:

- **Alignment with Market Trends:** Develop a strategy that aligns with current market trends and anticipates future shifts.
- **Innovation Integration:** Integrate innovation into the strategic vision to foster adaptability and competitiveness.
- **Customer-Centric Approach:** Center the strategic vision around meeting and exceeding customer expectations.3. **Resource Allocation: Maximizing Efficiency**

The Challenge: Without a plan, resource allocation becomes haphazard. Small businesses may struggle to identify where resources are most needed, leading to inefficiencies.

Strategies:

- **Budgeting:** Develop a detailed budget that allocates resources to different departments and initiatives.
- **Prioritization:** Prioritize initiatives based on their alignment with strategic goals and potential impact on business success.
- **Performance Metrics:** Implement performance metrics to assess the effectiveness of resource allocation.

3. Decision-Making Roadmap: From Chaos to Clarity

The Challenge: Decisions made without a strategic framework lack coherence and may not contribute to long-term success. A clear roadmap aids in making informed and goal-oriented decisions.

Strategies:

- **Decision-Making Protocols:** Establish protocols for decision-making that align with the overall strategic vision.
- **Risk Assessment:** Integrate risk assessment into decision-making processes, considering potential impacts on strategic goals.
- **Cross-Functional Collaboration:** Foster collaboration across departments to ensure decisions align with the broader organizational strategy.

4. Setting Realistic Growth Goals: A Steady Ascent

The Challenge: Lack of planning often results in unrealistic expectations. Setting unattainable goals can lead to frustration and disillusionment within the organization.

Strategies:

- **SMART Goals:** Set Specific, Measurable, Achievable, Relevant, and Time-bound goals that are aligned with the strategic vision.
- **Benchmarking:** Benchmark performance against industry standards to ensure goals are realistic and competitive.
- **Iterative Planning:** Embrace an iterative planning process that allows for adjustments based on evolving circumstances.

5. Adaptability: A Pivotal Component of Planning

The Challenge: Rigid plans can become obsolete in the face of unforeseen challenges. Businesses need to build adaptability into their planning processes.

Strategies:

- **Scenario Planning:** Develop scenarios that consider a range of potential future outcomes and plan accordingly.
- **Agile Methodologies:** Adopt agile methodologies that allow for flexibility and rapid adjustments to changing conditions.
- **Continuous Monitoring:** Regularly monitor key performance indicators and market dynamics to inform strategic adjustments.

6. Communication of the Plan: A Shared Vision

The Challenge: Even the most well-crafted plan is ineffective if it's not communicated effectively throughout the organization. Lack of communication leads to a lack of alignment.

Strategies:

- **Transparent Communication:** Share the strategic plan transparently with all stakeholders, fostering a sense of ownership.
- **Employee Training:** Provide training to ensure that employees understand their roles in executing the strategic plan.
- **Feedback Mechanisms:** Establish mechanisms for gathering feedback and insights from employees to refine the plan.

7. **Technology Integration: Enhancing Planning Efficiencies**
The Challenge: In today's digital age, businesses that fail to leverage technology in their planning processes risk falling behind.

Strategies:
- **Digital Planning Tools:** Utilize digital planning tools and software for streamlined collaboration and data analysis.
- **Data-Driven Insights:** Harness the power of data analytics to gain insights into market trends and consumer behavior.
- **Cybersecurity Measures:** Implement robust cybersecurity measures to protect sensitive planning data.

CONCLUSION: GUIDING THE SHIP WITH PURPOSE

In the ever-evolving business landscape, planning and strategy are the guiding stars that illuminate the path forward. Small businesses that invest time and effort in crafting comprehensive plans, aligning them with strategic visions, and fostering adaptability are better positioned to not only navigate challenges but to thrive and achieve sustained success. As the saying goes, "Failing to plan is planning to fail." It's time for small businesses to chart their course with purpose, resilience, and a strategic compass.

INADEQUATE MARKETING AND SALES

Crafting a Roadmap to Visibility and Revenue

Inadequate marketing and sales strategies can leave businesses in the shadows, struggling to connect with their target audience and generate essential revenue. Let's delve into the critical aspects of marketing and sales, exploring how small businesses can build visibility and robust revenue streams to secure sustainable success.

1. Understanding Customer Demographics: The Foundation of Marketing

The Challenge: Without a deep understanding of customer demographics, businesses may struggle to tailor their marketing messages effectively. Generic campaigns often miss the mark, resulting in a lack of engagement.

Strategies:
- **Market Research:** Invest in comprehensive market research to understand the needs, preferences, and behaviors of the target audience.
- **Buyer Personas:** Develop detailed buyer personas to humanize and personalize marketing strategies.

- **Feedback Loops:** Establish feedback mechanisms to continuously refine customer understanding and adapt strategies accordingly.

2. Robust Marketing Campaigns: Breaking Through the Noise

The Challenge: In a crowded digital landscape, generic or lackluster marketing campaigns are easily drowned out. Building visibility requires robust, targeted efforts that capture attention.

Strategies:
- **Multichannel Presence:** Embrace a multichannel marketing approach, leveraging platforms that align with the target audience.
- **Content Marketing:** Develop valuable and shareable content that establishes the business as an industry authority.
- **Consistent Branding:** Ensure consistency in branding across all marketing channels for instant recognition.

3. Investing Adequate Budget in Marketing: The Lifeline for Visibility

The Challenge: Allocating insufficient budget to marketing limits the reach and impact of campaigns. Many small businesses underestimate the critical role marketing plays in driving growth.

Strategies:
- **Budget Allocation:** Dedicate a reasonable percentage of the overall budget to marketing efforts, recognizing it as an investment rather than an expense.

- **ROI Tracking:** Implement systems to track the return on investment (ROI) from marketing expenditures, allowing for data-driven adjustments.
- **Strategic Partnerships:** Explore cost-effective marketing strategies through partnerships with complementary businesses or influencers.

4. Sales Tactics Refinement: Turning Leads into Customers

The Challenge: Ineffective sales tactics can hinder the conversion of leads into customers. Small businesses need to continuously refine their sales approaches to align with customer expectations.

Strategies:
- **Sales Training:** Provide ongoing training for sales teams to enhance their skills and adapt to changing market dynamics.
- **Customer-Centric Approach:** Prioritize a customer-centric approach in sales, focusing on understanding customer needs and providing tailored solutions.
- **Utilize Technology:** Integrate sales automation tools and customer relationship management (CRM) systems to streamline processes and enhance efficiency.

5. Personalization in Marketing: A Tailored Approach

The Challenge: Generic marketing messages often fall flat. Personalization is key to capturing the attention and loyalty of potential customers.

Strategies:
- **Data Utilization:** Leverage customer data to create personalized marketing messages and offers.

- **Behavioral Targeting:** Implement behavioral targeting strategies to deliver content and promotions based on customer actions and preferences.
- **Segmentation:** Divide the audience into segments and tailor marketing messages to address the specific needs and interests of each segment.

6. Harnessing the Power of AI in Marketing: A Cautionary Note

The Challenge: While AI presents opportunities for enhanced marketing, it's not a one-size-fits-all solution. Businesses must approach AI with caution, understanding its capabilities and limitations.

Strategies:

- **Educate Teams:** Ensure marketing teams have a solid understanding of AI applications and limitations.
- **Supervised Implementation:** Implement AI tools under the supervision of experienced professionals to prevent unintended consequences.
- **Continuous Monitoring:** Regularly monitor and analyze AI-generated insights to ensure they align with broader marketing goals.

7. Community Engagement: Beyond Transactions to Relationships

The Challenge: Focusing solely on transactions can hinder long-term customer relationships. Small businesses must prioritize community engagement to build loyalty.

Strategies:

- **Social Media Presence:** Actively engage with the audience on social media, responding to comments, messages, and participating in conversations.
- **Customer Feedback Integration:** Use customer feedback to make improvements and demonstrate responsiveness.
- **Community Events:** Organize or participate in community events to strengthen connections with local customers.

8. Continuous Learning in Marketing: Staying Ahead

The Challenge: The marketing landscape evolves rapidly. Small businesses need to foster a culture of continuous learning to stay ahead of trends and competitors.

Strategies:

- **Training Programs:** Provide ongoing training programs to keep marketing teams abreast of new technologies, strategies, and best practices.
- **Industry Networking:** Encourage participation in industry events, conferences, and forums to stay connected with the latest developments.
- **Metrics Analysis:** Regularly analyze marketing metrics to identify areas for improvement and optimization.

CONCLUSION: ILLUMINATING THE PATH TO SUCCESS

Inadequate marketing and sales are like operating a lighthouse without a beacon - businesses remain unseen in the vast sea of competition. By understanding customer demographics, investing in robust marketing campaigns, allocating adequate budget, refining sales tactics, personalizing marketing approaches, approaching AI with caution, prioritizing community engagement, and fostering continuous learning, small businesses can illuminate their path to success. Visibility and revenue streams are not mere byproducts of effective marketing and sales; they are the lifelines that sustain businesses in a dynamic and competitive landscape.

OPERATIONAL INEFFICIENCIES

Navigating the Stream for Sustainable Growth

Operational inefficiencies are akin to navigating turbulent waters with a leaky vessel. To achieve sustainable growth, small businesses must not only plug the leaks but also streamline their operational processes. Let's explore the critical aspects of operational efficiency and how businesses can navigate the stream for growth.

1. **Process Optimization: The Backbone of Efficiency**
   The Challenge: Poorly defined or outdated processes can be a significant source of operational inefficiencies. Streamlining processes is foundational to improving overall efficiency.

Strategies:
- **Process Audits:** Conduct regular audits to identify bottlenecks, redundancies, and areas for improvement.
- **Automation Integration:** Implement automation tools to streamline routine and repetitive tasks.
- **Continuous Improvement:** Foster a culture of continuous improvement, encouraging teams to suggest and implement process enhancements.

2. Supply Chain Management: From Weaknesses to Strengths

The Challenge: Ineffective supply chain management can lead to delays, excess inventory, and increased costs. Small businesses must assess and optimize their supply chain for efficiency.

Strategies:

- **Supplier Collaboration:** Collaborate closely with suppliers to optimize ordering processes and reduce lead times.
- **Inventory Management:** Implement just-in-time inventory practices to minimize holding costs and prevent overstocking.
- **Risk Mitigation:** Develop contingency plans for potential supply chain disruptions and diversify suppliers when feasible.

3. Benchmarking Against Industry Standards: The Yardstick for Efficiency

The Challenge: Small businesses may lack benchmarks for gauging their operational efficiency. Comparing performance against industry standards provides valuable insights and identifies areas for improvement.

Strategies:

- **Industry Research:** Stay informed about industry best practices and benchmarks related to operational efficiency.
- **Key Performance Indicators (KPIs):** Develop and monitor KPIs that align with industry standards to track and measure operational performance.
- **Competitor Analysis:** Regularly analyze competitors to identify operational strategies that contribute to their success.

4. Technology Integration: Efficiency Amplified

The Challenge: Failure to leverage technology in operations can result in manual errors, inefficiencies, and missed opportunities for improvement. Small businesses need to embrace technology for enhanced efficiency.

Strategies:

- **Digital Collaboration Tools:** Utilize digital collaboration tools to enhance communication and project management.
- **Enterprise Resource Planning (ERP) Systems:** Implement ERP systems to streamline various aspects of business operations.
- **Data Analytics:** Leverage data analytics for insights into operational performance and areas for optimization.

5. Employee Training and Empowerment: The Human Element

The Challenge: Employees unaware of efficient processes or lacking empowerment may inadvertently contribute to operational inefficiencies. Training and empowering the workforce are crucial components.

Strategies:

- **Comprehensive Training Programs:** Provide ongoing training programs to ensure employees are familiar with efficient processes and tools.
- **Empowerment Culture:** Encourage employees to take ownership of their roles and contribute ideas for operational improvements.
- **Feedback Mechanisms:** Establish channels for employees to provide feedback on operational processes and suggest enhancements.

6. Lean Methodology: Efficiency at Its Core

The Challenge: Excess waste in processes can hinder efficiency. Adopting lean methodologies, which focus on eliminating waste and optimizing value, can lead to significant improvements.

Strategies:

- **Waste Identification:** Identify and eliminate various forms of waste, including time, materials, and resources.
- **Continuous Flow Processes:** Implement processes that enable a continuous and smooth flow of operations.
- **Kaizen Philosophy:** Embrace the Kaizen philosophy of continuous improvement, encouraging small, incremental changes over time.

7. Customer-Centric Operations: The Heart of Efficiency

The Challenge: Operational efficiency should align with customer expectations. A misalignment can result in dissatisfaction and potential loss of business.

Strategies:

- **Customer Feedback Integration:** Use customer feedback to identify areas where operational improvements can enhance satisfaction.
- **Agile Operations:** Foster agility in operations to respond quickly to changing customer demands.
- **Real-Time Communication:** Ensure real-time communication channels to address customer concerns promptly.

8. **Environmental Sustainability: Efficiency Beyond Profit**
The Challenge: Efficiency is not only about profit but also about sustainability. Implementing environmentally friendly practices can contribute to both operational efficiency and social responsibility.

Strategies:
- **Green Practices:** Integrate environmentally sustainable practices into operational processes.
- **Energy Efficiency:** Implement energy-efficient technologies and practices to reduce costs and environmental impact.
- **Supplier Sustainability:** Collaborate with suppliers who adhere to environmentally friendly practices.

CONCLUSION: NAVIGATING THE STREAM WITH PRECISION

In the journey toward sustainable growth, operational efficiency is the compass that guides small businesses through the stream. By optimizing processes, enhancing supply chain management, benchmarking against industry standards, embracing technology, investing in employee training and empowerment, adopting lean methodologies, prioritizing customer-centric operations, and integrating environmentally sustainable practices, businesses can navigate the stream with precision and purpose. Operational efficiency is not a one-time achievement but an ongoing commitment to continuous improvement and adaptation to ever-changing waters. As the saying goes, "Efficiency is doing things right; effectiveness is doing the right things." In the realm of small business operations, doing both right is the key to sustained success.

REGULATORY COMPLIANCE ISSUES

Safeguarding Business Integrity in the Legal Landscape

Navigating the complex regulatory landscape is akin to steering a ship through turbulent waters. Small businesses must proactively address regulatory compliance to avoid legal risks and liabilities that can jeopardize their integrity and operations. Let's delve into the critical aspects of regulatory compliance and explore strategies for navigating the legal landscape.

1. **Understanding Regulatory Landscape: The Foundation of Compliance**

   The Challenge: A lack of understanding of the regulatory landscape can expose businesses to inadvertent violations. Small businesses need to comprehend the specific regulations governing their industry.

Strategies:
- **Legal Consultation:** Seek legal advice to understand industry-specific regulations and compliance requirements.

- **Regular Updates:** Stay informed about changes in regulations through industry publications, legal updates, and professional networks.
- **Internal Compliance Teams:** Establish internal teams responsible for monitoring and interpreting regulatory changes.

2. Compliance Programs: A Proactive Shield

The Challenge: Without a structured compliance program, businesses may struggle to systematically address regulatory requirements. Proactive measures are essential for creating a shield against legal challenges.

Strategies:
- **Compliance Audits:** Conduct regular compliance audits to assess adherence to regulatory standards.
- **Documented Policies:** Develop comprehensive policies and procedures that align with regulatory requirements.
- **Employee Training:** Provide ongoing training to employees to ensure awareness of compliance obligations.

3. Data Protection and Privacy: Guarding Against Vulnerabilities

The Challenge: In an era of increasing data privacy concerns, businesses must navigate and comply with data protection regulations. Mishandling personal information can lead to severe legal consequences.

Strategies:
- **Data Security Measures:** Implement robust data security measures to protect sensitive information.

- **Privacy Policies:** Develop and communicate clear privacy policies outlining how customer data is managed.
- **GDPR Compliance:** If applicable, ensure compliance with the General Data Protection Regulation (GDPR) or other regional data protection laws.

4. Contractual Compliance: Mitigating Legal Risks

The Challenge: Failure to comply with contractual obligations can result in legal disputes. Small businesses must diligently review and adhere to contractual agreements.

Strategies:

- **Legal Review:** Involve legal professionals in the review and negotiation of contracts.
- **Contract Management Systems:** Implement systems for managing contracts, deadlines, and renewal dates.
- **Open Communication:** Establish transparent communication channels with business partners to address potential compliance issues.

5. Workplace Regulations: Nurturing a Healthy Work Environment

The Challenge: Compliance with labor laws and workplace regulations is critical for maintaining a healthy and lawful work environment. Failure to do so can result in legal and reputational damage.

Strategies:

- **Human Resources Compliance Training:** Train human resources personnel on labor laws and workplace regulations.

- **Employee Handbook:** Develop a comprehensive employee handbook outlining rights, responsibilities, and company policies.
- **Fair Employment Practices:** Adhere to fair employment practices, including equal opportunity and non-discrimination policies.

6. Environmental Compliance: Balancing Business and Ecology

The Challenge: Businesses must align their operations with environmental regulations to minimize ecological impact. Non-compliance can lead to fines and damage to the brand's reputation.

Strategies:

- **Environmental Impact Assessments:** Conduct assessments to identify and mitigate environmental impacts.
- **Green Practices:** Integrate sustainable and eco-friendly practices into operational processes.
- **Regulatory Monitoring:** Stay updated on environmental regulations and adjust practices accordingly.

7. Financial Regulations: Upholding Fiscal Integrity

The Challenge: Adherence to financial regulations is paramount for fiscal integrity. Failure to comply with financial laws can lead to audits, penalties, and reputational damage.

Strategies:

- **Accounting Best Practices:** Follow industry-accepted accounting principles and standards.

- **Financial Audits:** Conduct regular financial audits to ensure compliance with regulatory requirements.
- **Tax Compliance:** Stay informed about tax regulations and file accurate and timely tax returns.

8. Crisis Management and Response Plans: Preparing for Legal Challenges

The Challenge: Legal challenges can arise unexpectedly. Having crisis management and response plans in place is crucial for mitigating the impact of legal issues.

Strategies:

- **Legal Counsel Retention:** Retain legal counsel to provide immediate advice in the event of a legal challenge.
- **Communication Protocols:** Establish clear communication protocols for addressing legal issues both internally and externally.
- **Document Retention:** Maintain organized records and documents to facilitate legal responses.

CONCLUSION: SAILING THE LEGAL SEAS WITH CONFIDENCE

Regulatory compliance is the compass that guides businesses through the legal seas. By understanding the regulatory landscape, implementing proactive compliance programs, safeguarding data protection and privacy, ensuring contractual compliance, nurturing a healthy workplace, aligning with environmental regulations, upholding financial integrity, and preparing for legal challenges with crisis management and response plans, small businesses can sail confidently through the legal landscape. Compliance is not merely a legal obligation; it is a commitment to ethical business practices, reputation preservation, and long-term sustainability. As small businesses navigate the legal seas, adherence to regulatory standards becomes the wind in their sails, propelling them toward success.

TECHNOLOGY CHALLENGES

Embracing the Digital Imperative for Small Businesses

In the ever-evolving landscape of technology, businesses face a critical imperative: adapt or risk obsolescence. For small businesses, embracing technology is not just a matter of survival but an avenue for enhanced efficiency, improved customer experiences, and sustained competitiveness. Let's delve into the challenges posed by technology and explore strategies for small businesses to navigate the digital landscape.

1. **Technological Adoption vs. Obsolescence: The Strategic Dilemma**

   The Challenge: The rapid pace of technological change can make it challenging for small businesses to determine the right time to adopt new technologies. Delaying adoption may lead to obsolescence, while premature adoption may strain resources.

Strategies:
- **Technology Roadmaps:** Develop long-term technology roadmaps aligned with business goals.
- **Scalability Considerations:** Choose technologies that allow for scalable adoption as the business grows.

- **Industry Benchmarks:** Stay informed about industry benchmarks and emerging technologies relevant to the business.

2. Integration of Technology with Operations: A Seamless Connection

The Challenge: Integrating technology seamlessly with existing operations is crucial for realizing its benefits. Poor integration can lead to inefficiencies and operational disruptions.

Strategies:

- **Comprehensive Planning:** Plan technology integration comprehensively, involving all relevant departments.
- **Employee Training:** Provide training to employees to ensure they are proficient in using new technologies.
- **Continuous Evaluation:** Regularly evaluate the performance of integrated technologies and make adjustments as needed.

3. Customer Service and Technological Investment: A Symbiotic Relationship

The Challenge: The lack of technological investment can hamper customer service in numerous ways, from communication inefficiencies to inadequate support systems.

Strategies:

- **Customer-Centric Technologies:** Invest in technologies that enhance the customer experience, such as chatbots, CRM systems, and personalized communication tools.
- **Maximized Budgets:** Allocate budgets that allow for maximum technological spending, understanding the

return on investment (ROI) in terms of improved customer satisfaction and loyalty.

- **Real-Time Support:** Implement real-time support systems to address customer queries promptly and efficiently.

4. Cybersecurity Concerns: Safeguarding Digital Assets

The Challenge: As businesses embrace technology, the risk of cybersecurity threats increases. Small businesses may lack the robust cybersecurity measures necessary to protect sensitive digital assets.

Strategies:

- **Cybersecurity Training:** Train employees on cybersecurity best practices to prevent breaches.
- **Investment in Security:** Allocate resources to invest in robust cybersecurity measures, including firewalls, encryption, and secure authentication.
- **Regular Audits:** Conduct regular cybersecurity audits to identify vulnerabilities and address them proactively.

5. Digital Marketing and Online Presence: Navigating the Virtual Marketplace

The Challenge: The virtual marketplace requires a strong online presence and effective digital marketing strategies. Small businesses that neglect digital marketing may struggle to reach their target audience.

Strategies:

- **Responsive Websites:** Ensure websites are mobile-friendly and responsive to enhance the online user experience.

- **Social Media Engagement:** Leverage social media platforms for marketing and customer engagement.
- **SEO Strategies:** Implement search engine optimization (SEO) strategies to improve online visibility.

6. Data Management and Analysis: Unlocking Insights

The Challenge: The abundance of data can be overwhelming for small businesses. Without proper data management and analysis, valuable insights may remain untapped.

Strategies:
- **Data Analytics Tools:** Invest in data analytics tools to extract meaningful insights from collected data.
- **Data Governance Policies:** Establish data governance policies to ensure the responsible and secure handling of customer information.
- **Actionable Insights:** Transform data into actionable insights that inform business decisions and strategies.

7. Cloud Computing and Scalability: A Technological Paradigm

The Challenge: Traditional infrastructure may limit scalability. Adopting cloud computing allows businesses to scale operations flexibly, but the transition must be carefully managed.

Strategies:
- **Gradual Transition:** Transition to cloud computing gradually, ensuring that existing systems are compatible.
- **Cost-Benefit Analysis:** Conduct a thorough cost-benefit analysis to determine the financial viability of cloud solutions.

- **Security Protocols:** Implement robust security protocols when adopting cloud services to safeguard sensitive data.

8. Technology Training and Upskilling: Empowering the Workforce

The Challenge: The adoption of new technologies necessitates a skilled workforce. Without proper training and upskilling, employees may struggle to leverage technological tools effectively.

Strategies:

- **Training Programs:** Develop ongoing training programs to keep employees updated on technological advancements.
- **Skill Assessments:** Regularly assess employee skill levels and provide targeted training where needed.
- **Employee Involvement:** Involve employees in the selection process of new technologies to ensure buy-in and a smoother transition.

CONCLUSION: FORGING A DIGITAL PATH TO SUCCESS

In the age of the digital imperative, small businesses must not view technology as a challenge but as a pathway to success. By strategically navigating technological adoption, seamlessly integrating it with operations, investing in customer-centric technologies, prioritizing cybersecurity, embracing digital marketing, mastering data management and analysis, leveraging cloud computing for scalability, and empowering the workforce through training and upskilling, businesses can forge a digital path that aligns with their goals. Technology is not just a tool; it's a dynamic force that propels businesses toward innovation, efficiency, and sustained relevance in the digital age. As small businesses embrace the digital imperative, they embark on a transformative journey that transcends challenges and leads to a future of digital prosperity.

ECONOMIC DOWNTURNS

Navigating Turbulent Waters for Small Businesses

Economic downturns are a formidable challenge for businesses, and small enterprises, with limited financial reserves, face unique hurdles during turbulent times. To weather economic storms successfully, small businesses must employ strategic measures such as diversifying revenue streams, practicing prudent financial management, and demonstrating the ability to pivot in response to challenging economic conditions. Let's explore these essential survival strategies in greater detail.

1. Diversification of Revenue Streams: Building Resilience

The Challenge: Over-reliance on a single revenue source can leave businesses vulnerable during economic downturns. Diversifying revenue streams is crucial for building resilience and reducing exposure to economic fluctuations.

Strategies:
- **Product and Service Expansion:** Explore opportunities to expand the range of products or services offered.
- **Targeting New Markets:** Identify and enter new markets to broaden the customer base.

- **Subscription Models:** Introduce subscription-based models to create steady, recurring revenue.

2. **Prudent Financial Management: Building a Solid Foundation**
The Challenge: Effective financial management is the bedrock of small business resilience during economic downturns. Prudent financial practices help conserve resources and provide a financial cushion during challenging times.

Strategies:
- **Cash Flow Monitoring:** Regularly monitor and analyze cash flow to identify potential issues early.
- **Cost Cutting:** Implement cost-cutting measures, focusing on non-essential expenditures.
- **Emergency Funds:** Establish and maintain emergency funds to cover operational expenses during downturns.

3. **Pivoting During Economic Challenges: A Strategic Shift**
The Challenge: The ability to pivot strategically is a defining trait of businesses that survive economic downturns. Pivoting involves adapting products, services, or operations to align with changing market demands and conditions.

Strategies:
- **Market Research:** Conduct thorough market research to identify emerging trends and changing consumer behavior.
- **Agile Decision-Making:** Foster an agile decision-making process that allows for quick responses to market dynamics.
- **Innovative Offerings:** Introduce innovative products or services that cater to current market needs.

4. Customer Relationship Management: Fostering Loyalty

The Challenge: Maintaining strong customer relationships is critical during economic downturns. Customer loyalty can be a stabilizing force that sustains a business through challenging times.

Strategies:

- **Communication Transparency:** Communicate openly with customers about challenges the business is facing and steps being taken to address them.
- **Customer Incentives:** Offer promotions, discounts, or loyalty programs to incentivize continued patronage.
- **Personalized Engagement:** Personalize customer engagement to create a sense of connection and loyalty.

5. Strategic Partnerships and Collaborations: Sharing Resources

The Challenge: Strategic partnerships and collaborations can provide small businesses with shared resources, expertise, and a broader customer base. These alliances are particularly valuable during economic downturns.

Strategies:

- **Identifying Synergies:** Seek partnerships with businesses that complement rather than compete.
- **Cost-Sharing Arrangements:** Explore cost-sharing arrangements that reduce financial burdens for all parties involved.
- **Joint Marketing Initiatives:** Collaborate on marketing initiatives to reach a wider audience.

6. **Agile Workforce Management: Adapting Human Resources**
   The Challenge: Adapting the workforce to economic challenges is a delicate but necessary process. Small businesses must balance operational needs with employee well-being.

Strategies:
- **Cross-Training:** Cross-train employees to manage multiple roles, increasing flexibility.
- **Flexible Work Arrangements:** Implement flexible work arrangements to accommodate changing business needs.
- **Open Communication:** Maintain transparent communication with the workforce about challenges and potential changes.

7. **Government Assistance Exploration: Leveraging Support**
   The Challenge: Government assistance programs are often available during economic downturns. Small businesses should explore and leverage these resources to mitigate financial strains.

Strategies:
- **Researching Programs:** Stay informed about government assistance programs and eligibility criteria.
- **Timely Applications:** Apply for assistance programs in a timely manner to ensure access to available support.
- **Tax Relief Utilization:** Explore tax relief measures and take advantage of any applicable incentives.

8. **Scenario Planning: Preparing for Uncertainty**
   The Challenge: Uncertainty is a hallmark of economic downturns. Scenario planning involves preparing for

various potential outcomes and developing strategies to address each scenario.

Strategies:
- **Risk Assessments:** Conduct thorough risk assessments to identify potential challenges and their impact.
- **Contingency Plans:** Develop contingency plans for different economic scenarios, including revenue decline and market volatility.
- **Regular Review:** Periodically review and update scenario plans to align with evolving economic conditions.

CONCLUSION: SAILING THROUGH ECONOMIC STORMS

In the unpredictable waters of economic downturns, small businesses can navigate successfully by embracing strategies that enhance resilience, agility, and adaptability. Diversifying revenue streams, practicing prudent financial management, pivoting strategically, fostering customer relationships, engaging in strategic partnerships, adapting workforce management, exploring government assistance, and engaging in scenario planning are the sails that propel businesses through economic storms. As small businesses face challenges, these strategic measures become not only survival tactics but also the compass guiding them toward sustained success. The journey through economic downturns is an opportunity for growth, innovation, and the fortification of business foundations. As the saying goes, "Smooth seas do not make skillful sailors," and it is during economic challenges that the true mettle of small businesses is assessed and strengthened.

FAILURE TO PIVOT

The Imperative of Embracing Change for Business Survival

In the dynamic landscape of business, change is not just inevitable; it is the lifeblood of sustained relevance and success. Industries evolve, consumer preferences shift, and technologies advance, demanding that businesses adapt or risk becoming obsolete. For small businesses, which often operate in nimble ecosystems, the ability to pivot is not just an advantage but a survival necessity. Let's explore the critical aspects of embracing change for business survival and why a reluctance to pivot can be detrimental.

1. **Understanding the Need to Pivot: The Pulse of Market Dynamics**

   The Challenge: Business landscapes are ever shifting, influenced by technological advancements, economic trends, and changing consumer behaviors. Small businesses that fail to recognize the need to pivot risk falling behind.

Strategies:
- **Market Research:** Conduct regular market research to identify emerging trends, competitive movements, and shifts in consumer preferences.

- **Monitoring Indicators:** Stay vigilant about key performance indicators (KPIs) and market signals that may indicate the necessity for change.
- **Competitor Analysis:** Continuously analyze the strategies and successes of competitors to identify areas for improvement and innovation.

2. Agility and Responsiveness: The Small Business Advantage

The Challenge: Small businesses possess the advantage of agility and responsiveness. Failing to leverage this nimbleness to adapt quickly to market shifts can hinder competitiveness.

Strategies:
- **Cross-Functional Collaboration:** Foster collaboration across different departments to ensure a collective understanding of market dynamics and the need for change.
- **Streamlined Decision-Making:** Maintain streamlined decision-making processes that allow for quick responses to changing circumstances.
- **Agile Workforce:** Cultivate an agile workforce that is adaptable and open to change, encouraging innovation from all levels.

3. Recognizing Stagnation: The Silent Business Killer

The Challenge: Stagnation, often accompanied by a reluctance to pivot, can be a silent business killer. Businesses that become complacent with their existing strategies risk losing their competitive edge.

Strategies:

- **Regular Evaluations:** Periodically evaluate business strategies, product offerings, and operational processes to identify signs of stagnation.
- **Customer Feedback:** Actively seek customer feedback to gauge satisfaction and identify areas for improvement.
- **Innovation Cultivation:** Foster a culture of innovation within the organization, encouraging employees to propose and implement new ideas.

4. Overcoming Resistance to Change: A Cultural Shift

The Challenge: Resistance to change can permeate organizational culture, hindering the ability to pivot effectively. Overcoming this resistance requires a concerted effort to instigate a cultural shift.

Strategies:

- **Transparent Communication:** Communicate openly about the reasons for change, emphasizing the benefits and opportunities it presents.
- **Inclusive Decision-Making:** Involve employees at various levels in the decision-making process to foster a sense of ownership and engagement.
- **Training and Development:** Provide training and resources to help employees develop the skills needed for new strategies and approaches.

5. Pivoting Strategies: Adapting with Purpose

The Challenge: Pivoting is not just about change for the sake of change; it's about adapting with purpose. Businesses must identify strategic pivots that align with long-term goals and market demands.

Strategies:

- **Strategic Planning:** Align pivots with the overarching business strategy, ensuring a cohesive approach.
- **Customer-Centric Pivots:** Base pivots on customer needs and preferences, aiming to enhance the customer experience.
- **Risk Assessment:** Conduct thorough risk assessments to understand the potential impact of pivots and mitigate associated challenges.

6. Learning from Failure: A Catalyst for Innovation

The Challenge: Fear of failure can paralyze businesses, preventing them from taking risks and embracing change. However, failure is often a catalyst for innovation and growth.

Strategies:

- **Fail Fast, Learn Faster:** Encourage a culture where failures are seen as opportunities to learn and improve.
- **Post-Mortem Analysis:** Conduct post-mortem analyses of unsuccessful initiatives to extract valuable insights for future endeavors.
- **Celebrating Innovation:** Recognize and celebrate successful innovations, creating a positive environment for experimentation.

7. Technology Integration: A Driving Force for Change

The Challenge: Technology is a powerful driver of change, and businesses that resist its integration may struggle to adapt to evolving market landscapes.

Strategies:

- **Tech Adoption Roadmaps:** Develop comprehensive roadmaps for the adoption of new technologies, ensuring they align with business goals.
- **Employee Training:** Invest in ongoing training programs to equip employees with the skills needed to leverage new technologies.
- **Continuous Tech Assessment:** Regularly assess the technological landscape to identify opportunities for integration and optimization.

8. Market Validation: Testing and Iterating

The Challenge: Before fully committing to a pivot, businesses must validate their ideas with the market. Failing to evaluate and iterate can lead to misguided pivots.

Strategies:

- **MVP Approach:** Embrace a Minimum Viable Product (MVP) approach to test new concepts quickly and gather feedback.
- **A/B Testing:** Conduct A/B testing for marketing strategies, product features, and other elements to identify the most effective approaches.
- **Iterative Development:** Iterate on products or services based on customer feedback and market validation results.

CONCLUSION: EMBRACING THE WINDS OF CHANGE

The ability to pivot is not just a survival mechanism; it's a strategic imperative for businesses navigating the dynamic seas of industry evolution. Small businesses possess a unique advantage in their nimbleness and agility, allowing them to adapt quickly to changing market conditions. By understanding the need to pivot, leveraging organizational agility, recognizing signs of stagnation, overcoming resistance to change, strategically planning pivots, embracing a culture of innovation, learning from failure, integrating technology, and validating ideas through market testing, businesses can navigate the challenges of change with purpose and resilience. Embracing the winds of change is not just about survival; it's about thriving in an environment where adaptability is the key to sustained success. As businesses pivot strategically, they harness the power of change to propel themselves toward innovation, growth, and long-term prosperity.

In the sophisticated tapestry of business success, few threads are as influential and delicate as the internal culture and team dynamics that permeate an organization. As the unseen architects of a company's foundation, these elements shape the very essence of its identity and resilience. A cohesive and vibrant internal culture, nurtured by robust team dynamics, serves as the bedrock upon which innovation, collaboration, and collective achievement flourish. This exploration takes us into the heart of organizational dynamics, where the pulse of success is not solely dictated by market forces but by the shared values, communication, and collaborative spirit within.

INTERNAL CULTURE AND TEAM DYNAMICS

The Foundation of Success

1. **Leadership Alignment:** The coherence of leadership in vision, values, and strategic direction is crucial. Misalignment among top leadership can lead to conflicting goals and ineffective decision-making.

2. **Team Morale and Motivation:** Low morale and lack of motivation among the workforce can hinder productivity and innovation. A disengaged team may not contribute to the best of its abilities, impacting overall business performance.

3. **Communication Breakdown:** Ineffective communication within the organization can lead to misunderstandings, unmet expectations, and a lack of clarity in roles and responsibilities.

Customer Service and Reputation Management: Building Trust in Turbulent Times

1. **Customer Service Quality:** Poor customer service, unresolved complaints, or consistently negative customer experiences can erode trust and drive customers away.

2. **Online Reputation Management:** Negative online reviews and a tarnished online reputation can significantly impact customer acquisition and retention.

Cybersecurity and Data Protection: Safeguarding Digital Assets

1. **Data Breaches and Loss:** In an increasingly digital age, inadequate cybersecurity measures can expose businesses to data breaches, leading to financial losses and reputational damage.

2. **Legal Consequences:** Non-compliance with data protection regulations can result in legal consequences and financial penalties.

Succession Planning and Business Continuity: Ensuring Longevity

1. **Succession Plan Absence:** Lack of a clear succession plan can disrupt business operations in the event of key personnel changes or unexpected departures.

2. **Inadequate Business Continuity Planning:** Failure to plan for unexpected disruptions, such as natural disasters or pandemics, can lead to severe business interruptions.

Environmental and Social Responsibility: The Role of Corporate Citizenship

1. **Sustainability Practices:** Increasingly, consumers value businesses with environmentally sustainable practices. Lack of commitment to sustainability may lead to a loss of market share.

2. **Social Responsibility:** Businesses that are not socially responsible or lack ethical practices may face backlash from consumers and stakeholders.

Technological Obsolescence: Staying Relevant in the Digital Era

1. **Lack of Technological Adaptation:** Failing to adopt new technologies or adapt to industry trends can render a business obsolete in a rapidly evolving market.

2. **Innovation Stagnation:** A lack of emphasis on innovation and staying ahead of technological advancements can hinder long-term competitiveness.

Global Economic Factors: Navigating Macroscopic Challenges

1. **Economic Downturns:** Beyond local factors, global economic shifts and recessions can significantly impact businesses, particularly those without diversification or contingency plans.

2. **Supply Chain Disruptions:** Dependence on a single-source supply chain or lack of resilience in the face of global disruptions can lead to operational challenges.

Intellectual Property Protection: Safeguarding Innovation

1. **Inadequate IP Protection:** Failure to protect intellectual property, such as patents, trademarks, or copyrights, can expose businesses to the risk of imitation and loss of competitive advantage.

2. **IP Litigation:** Legal battles over intellectual property can drain financial resources and distract from core business operations.

Regulatory Compliance: Navigating Legal Frameworks

1. **Changing Regulatory Landscape:** Failure to stay updated on industry regulations and adapt to changes in compliance requirements can lead to legal issues and financial penalties.

2. **Industry-Specific Compliance:** Different industries have unique regulatory frameworks, and non-compliance can result in severe consequences.

Market Saturation and Changing Trends: Staying Relevant

1. **Failure to Adapt to Trends:** Ignoring emerging market trends and consumer preferences can result in a loss of relevance and competitiveness.

2. **Increased Competition:** A saturated market with heightened competition can make it challenging for businesses to gain or maintain market share.

Mergers and Acquisitions: Navigating Strategic Moves

1. **Ineffective Integration:** Poorly managed mergers or acquisitions can lead to integration challenges, cultural clashes, and financial strain.

2. **Overleveraging:** Taking on excessive debt to fund mergers or acquisitions without a clear repayment plan can strain financial resources.

Psychological Factors: The Human Element in Business

1. **Founder's Dilemma:** A business's success may be closely tied to its founder, and burnout or a lack of succession planning can lead to failure.

2. **Decision-Making Biases:** Cognitive biases in decision-making, such as overconfidence or anchoring, can lead to poor strategic choices.

CONCLUSION: A HOLISTIC APPROACH TO UNDERSTANDING BUSINESS FAILURE

Business failure is rarely the result of a single factor but often a combination of internal and external elements. A holistic understanding of these critical aspects provides a nuanced perspective, empowering business owners to navigate challenges and foster resilience. In the subsequent chapters, we will delve into strategies and frameworks to address these multifaceted dynamics, offering a comprehensive guide to recognizing, preventing, and recovering from business failure.

In the intricate tapestry of business management, few challenges wield as much silent power as cash flow issues—a silent killer that stealthily erodes the financial stability of small and medium-sized enterprises (SMEs). As businesses navigate the dynamic landscapes of sales, purchasing, and operational demands, the web of funding solutions becomes a critical thread, woven intricately into the fabric of financial resilience. In this chapter, we embark on the exploration of cash flow issues, unraveling the tangled web that often ensnares businesses. From understanding the nuances of vendor and inventory management to unlocking a diverse array of funding solutions, our aim is not only to shed light on the intricacies of cash flow challenges but to equip SMEs with a comprehensive guide. For when the specter of cash flow instability looms, these solutions stand ready as vital tools, offering a lifeline to businesses in need of financial fortitude

UNLOCKING FINANCIAL RESILIENCE

A Comprehensive Exploration of Funding Solutions for SMEs

In the complex maneuvers of business endurance, cash flow emerges as a silent maestro, orchestrating the fate of small and medium-sized enterprises (SMEs). As businesses strive to navigate the complex financial terrain, a deeper exploration of funding solutions becomes imperative. This chapter delves into a myriad of financing options, unraveling the intricacies of each, while shedding light on collateral requirements and introducing prevailing private funding methods.

Traditional Bank Loans: A Pillar of Stability

Collateral: Traditional bank loans typically require collateral to secure the borrowed amount. Examples include real estate, equipment, or accounts receivable. The specific collateral may vary based on the loan terms and the financial institution's policies.

Private Funding Methods: While not strictly private, traditional bank loans offer stability and established structures. Their conventional nature aligns with more conservative investors seeking predictable returns.

Invoice Financing: Transforming Receivables into Liquidity

Collateral: Invoice financing itself is a collateralized form of funding, as the receivables function as security. The unpaid invoices serve as a guarantee, reducing the emphasis on additional collateral.

Private Funding Methods: Invoice financing aligns with private funding methods as it often involves specialized finance companies or platforms that cater to businesses seeking alternative financing beyond traditional banks.

Business Line of Credit: Navigating Financial Flexibility

Collateral: Business lines of credit may be secured or unsecured. Secured lines of credit often require collateral, which can include business assets, personal assets, or a blanket lien on business assets.

Private Funding Methods: Emerging private lenders and financial technology (fintech) platforms increasingly offer flexible lines of credit, catering to businesses with varying credit profiles and funding needs.

Merchant Cash Advances: Bridging Gaps with Future Sales

Collateral: Merchant cash advances are generally unsecured, meaning they don't require specific collateral. However, the repayment structure involves a percentage of daily credit card sales, serving as a de facto collateralized arrangement.

Private Funding Methods: Merchant cash advances are often facilitated by private lenders or alternative financing companies, emphasizing quick access to capital.

Peer-to-Peer (P2P) Lending: Crowdsourcing Financial Support

Collateral: P2P lending platforms may or may not require collateral, depending on the platform and the nature of the loan. Some loans may be unsecured, while others may involve collateralized arrangements.

Private Funding Methods: P2P lending epitomizes the shift towards private funding methods, as individual investors pool funds to provide financing to businesses in need.

Angel Investors: Infusing Capital with Expertise

Collateral: Angel investors typically invest in exchange for equity or convertible debt, meaning they gain a stake in the business. While not collateral in the traditional sense, this equity stake is a form of commitment and risk-sharing.

Private Funding Methods: Angel investors operate in the private domain, providing not just funds but also mentorship and industry expertise to businesses in which they invest.

Venture Capital (VC) Funding: Nurturing Growth with Strategic Backing

Collateral: Similar to angel investors, VC funding involves acquiring equity in the funded business. The equity stake serves as a form of collateral, aligning the interests of the venture capitalist with the success of the venture.

Private Funding Methods: Venture capitalists operate within private investment circles, focusing on high-growth potential businesses with the aim of substantial returns on investment.

Government Grants and Subsidies: Public Support for Strategic Initiatives

Collateral: Government grants and subsidies are typically non-repayable, meaning they don't require collateral. However, eligibility criteria and project-specific requirements may apply.

Private Funding Methods: While government-backed, these initiatives align with private funding methods as they often target specific industries or projects, providing financial support for strategic objectives.

Crowdfunding: Harnessing Collective Support

Collateral: Crowdfunding campaigns typically don't require collateral in the traditional sense. Backers contribute funds based on belief in the project rather than seeking collateral in return.

Private Funding Methods: Crowdfunding epitomizes the democratization of funding, utilizing online platforms to gather support from a broad audience.

Equipment Financing: Unlocking Capital for Asset Acquisition

Collateral: Equipment financing is inherently collateralized, as the equipment itself serves as security. If the business defaults, the lender can reclaim the financed equipment.

Private Funding Methods: While equipment financing can be offered by traditional banks, private lenders and specialized financing companies often cater to businesses seeking funds for specific equipment acquisitions.

Private Funding Evolution: Beyond Traditional Avenues

In addition to these established funding avenues, a growing landscape of private funding methods is shaping the financial future for SMEs. Private equity firms, family offices, and high-net-worth individuals are increasingly engaging with small businesses, providing not just capital but strategic guidance. Crowdsourced equity funding platforms allow businesses to reach a broader investor base, while revenue-based financing models align the interests of investors with a company's revenue trajectory.

Private Equity Firms: Strategic Backing for Growth

Private equity (PE) firms invest in businesses in exchange for equity ownership. Their involvement often extends beyond providing funds, as they actively participate in strategic decision-making to drive growth and enhance the value of their investments.

Family Offices: Personalized Investment Strategies

Family offices, representing high-net-worth individuals or families, are becoming influential players in SME financing. Their personalized approach allows for tailored investment strategies and long-term partnerships with businesses.

Crowdsourced Equity Funding: Broadening Investor Participation

Platforms like Seedrs, Crowdcube, and Republic enable businesses to raise capital by offering equity to a large pool of individual investors. This model democratizes investment, allowing businesses to secure funding from diverse backers.

Revenue-Based Financing: Aligning Interests for Success

In revenue-based financing, investors provide capital in exchange for a percentage of the business's future revenue. This model aligns the interests of investors with the success of the business, fostering a collaborative approach to growth.

Conclusion: Crafting a Financial Tapestry for Success

The financial landscape for SMEs is evolving, presenting a rich tapestry of funding solutions that extend beyond traditional boundaries. As businesses grapple with cash flow challenges, understanding the collateral requirements and exploring private funding methods becomes pivotal. Whether engaging with established financial institutions, alternative lenders, or private investors, SMEs have an array of options to navigate the intricate web of cash flow issues and unlock financial resilience.

CONCLUSION UNVEILING THE MOSAIC OF BUSINESS FAILURE:

In the intricate journey through the landscapes of business failure, we've traversed diverse terrains, unraveling the complexities woven into the very fabric of entrepreneurial endeavors. As we stand at the culmination of this exploration, it's crucial to reflect not only on the pitfalls but on the resilience and wisdom that emerges from dissecting failure.

A Mosaic of Insights: The analysis of business failure is akin to creating a mosaic, piece by piece, with each fragment representing a crucial aspect of the entrepreneurial journey. Financial analyses, operational metrics, market dynamics, and leadership evaluations are not isolated entities but interconnected elements that form a comprehensive picture. It's within the mosaic that the patterns of success and failure become discernible.

Beyond the Surface: Our quest delved deeper than the surface-level symptoms, uncovering the subtle nuances that often elude cursory examinations. Whether it's the emotional detachment required for objective decision-making, the cultural underpinnings of an organization, or the psychological factors shaping leadership, we've illuminated the layers beneath the obvious, acknowledging that business failure is rarely straightforward.

Frameworks for Resilience: While understanding failure is crucial, our journey is not a pessimistic one. Rather, it's a call to action informed by insights. We've equipped ourselves with frameworks — financial statement analyses, operational efficiency metrics, market analyses, and more — tools that transcend diagnosis to serve as instruments of resilience. These are the guiding stars for recalibrating, adapting, and steering towards a trajectory of sustainable success.

A Dynamic Landscape: The business landscape is dynamic, subject to the whims of economic shifts, technological revolutions, and societal changes. As we conclude, it's vital to embrace the understanding that failure is not a verdict but a punctuation mark in the ongoing narrative of business evolution. It's a call to reassess, learn, and pivot — an intrinsic part of entrepreneurial metamorphosis.

A Guide, Not an Epitaph: This exploration is not an epitaph but a guide, offering navigational tools for those at the helm of enterprises. In each failure lies an opportunity for introspection, reinvention, and a renewed commitment to crafting a resilient and adaptive business model.

Continual Adaptation: As we part ways, remember that the business landscape is ever evolving. The analysis models provided are not static formulas but living frameworks that demand continual adaptation. The lessons learned from one failure become the steppingstones to triumphs in the future.

Embracing Triumph through Tribulation: In the mosaic of business, triumph and tribulation coexist. It's the entrepreneur's ability to navigate both, to decipher the patterns within the mosaic of failure, which defines lasting success. Our hope is that this journey through analysis models serves as a beacon, guiding businesses not only through the storms but towards the shores of resilience and prosperity.

In the Tapestry of Business: As the final stroke in the tapestry of business, may the threads of failure not be seen as unraveling but as a vibrant part of the larger narrative. For in every unraveling, there lies the potential to weave a new story, one richer, wiser, and more resilient than before.

In this concluding chapter, we extend our sincerest wishes for your journey — a journey marked not only by the challenges that may arise but by the triumphs forged through the crucible of understanding, adaptability, and a relentless pursuit of excellence. May your entrepreneurial odyssey be defined by a mosaic where failure is but a fragment, and success, an ever-expanding masterpiece.

www.ingramcontent.com/pod-product-compliance
Lightning Source LLC
Chambersburg PA
CBHW071054290526
45795CB00004B/1487